Rookie Read-About® Geography

Maine

By Cynthia Walker

Consultants

Reading Adviser
Nanci R. Vargus, EdD
Assistant Professor of Literacy
University of Indianapolis, Indianapolis, Indiana

Subject Adviser
Charlene Smith Wagner
Children's Librarian
Gardiner Public Library
Gardiner, Maine

Children's Press®
A Division of Scholastic Inc.
New York   Toronto   London   Auckland   Sydney
Mexico City   New Delhi   Hong Kong
Danbury, Connecticut

Designer: Herman Adler Design
Photo Researcher: Caroline Anderson
The photo on the cover shows Stonington, Maine.

Library of Congress Cataloging-in-Publication Data

Walker, Cynthia.
  Maine / by Cynthia Walker.
      p. cm. — (Rookie read-about geography)
  Includes index.
  ISBN 0-516-25255-0 (lib. bdg.)   0-516-25157-0 (pbk.)
  1. Maine—Juvenile literature. 2. Maine—Geography—Juvenile literature.
  I. Title. II. Series.
  F19.3.W35 2005
  917.41'02—dc22   2005002090

CHILDREN'S PRESS, and ROOKIE READ-ABOUT®,
and associated logos are trademarks and/or registered trademarks
of Scholastic Library Publishing. SCHOLASTIC and associated logos
are trademarks and/or registered trademarks of Scholastic Inc.

1 2 3 4 5 6 7 8 9 10 R 14 13 12 11 10 09 08 07 06 05

Do you know what state is nicknamed the Pine Tree State?

Maine is the Pine
Tree State!

Maine has many tall trees.

Can you find Maine on
this map? It is in the
Northeast.

CANADA

WASHINGTON
OREGON
MONTANA
NORTH DAKOTA
MINNESOTA
NEW HAMPSHIRE
VERMONT
MAINE
IDAHO
WYOMING
SOUTH DAKOTA
WISCONSIN
MICHIGAN
NEW YORK
MASSACHUSETTS
RHODE ISLAND
CONNECTICUT
NEBRASKA
IOWA
PENNSYLVANIA
NEW JERSEY
NEVADA
UTAH
COLORADO
KANSAS
ILLINOIS
INDIANA
OHIO
WEST VIRGINIA
DELAWARE
MARYLAND
Washington, D.C.
CALIFORNIA
MISSOURI
KENTUCKY
VIRGINIA
ARIZONA
NEW MEXICO
OKLAHOMA
ARKANSAS
TENNESSEE
NORTH CAROLINA
SOUTH CAROLINA
TEXAS
MISSISSIPPI
ALABAMA
GEORGIA
LOUISIANA
FLORIDA

North
West East
South

ALASKA CANADA

MEXICO

HAWAII

5

Maine has mountains, forests, lakes, and a rocky coastline.

The highest mountain in Maine is Mount Katahdin. It is 5,267 feet tall.

Hiking and rock climbing
are fun things to do
in Maine.

People also like sailing and white-water rafting.

Maine became the 23rd state in 1820. Before that, it was a part of Massachusetts.

This is Maine's state flag.

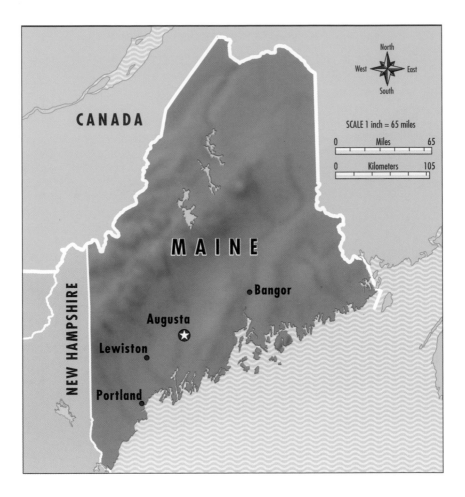

Augusta is Maine's state capital. Portland is the largest city in Maine.

Lewiston and Bangor are other major cities.

In Maine, some people fish or farm. Others work in offices, ski resorts, and parks.

This man catches lobster.

This farmer is picking blueberries.

Farmers in Maine grow potatoes, broccoli, and blueberries.

Moose, black bears, red squirrels, and other wild animals live in Maine.

This is a moose.

The state bird is the chickadee.

Maine is cold in the winter. Some people like to cross-country ski in the snow.

Maine is warm in the summer. During the summer, people enjoy the beach.

What would you like
to do in Maine?

Words You Know

blueberries

chickadee

coastline

moose

Mt. Katahdin

rafting

skiing

31

Index

About the Author

Cynthia Walker is an author and illustrator of children's books. She loves to travel and explore exciting places. She lives in New York.

Photo Credits

Photographs © 2005: AP/Wide World Photos/Pat Wellenbach: 25, 31 bottom right; Corbis Images: 3 (Neil Rabinowitz), 23, 30 top right (Lynda Richardson), 20, 30 top left (David H. Wells); David J. Forbert: cover; Dembinsky Photo Assoc./Claudia Adams: 22, 31 top left; Index Stock Imagery/Paul Johnson: 12, 31 bottom left; Nance S. Trueworthy: 26, 29; Photo Researchers, NY/George Rananlli: 9, 31 top right; The Image Works: 6, 30 bottom (Townsend P. Dickinson), 19 (Jeff Greenberg), 15 (Joe Sohm), 11 (Jim West).
Maps on pages 5, 16 by Bob Italiano